The Picture Book of

GRAINS

ANITA BROOKS

The John Day Company   New York

By Anita Brooks

THE PICTURE BOOK OF FISHERIES
THE PICTURE BOOK OF TEA AND COFFEE
THE PICTURE BOOK OF GRAINS

Library of Congress Catalogue Card Number: 62-10936

MANUFACTURED IN THE UNITED STATES OF AMERICA

Sixth Impression

PREFACE

The *Picture Book of Grains* was written with three purposes in mind. All, it is hoped, are expressed successfully enough to aid the young student both in knowledge and in growth.

The photographs and text are meant, primarily, to be informative. They tell what the various grains are and where they grow. They show what wheat, rye, barley, oats, rice, maize (corn), and doura look like, and how grain is harvested and transported. They point out the farmers' problems and explain some of the study and technical exchange that goes on in agriculture.

The second purpose is an attempt to show the world at work: a related and ever-fascinating world of fields and farms, wharves and warehouses, research and experiment, and of the people who raise, process, and ship man's most important food.

The third purpose is to illustrate the words of one of my professors, Bert James Loewenberg, that "the only self-sufficient unit is the world itself," and to suggest that within this unit, the interdependency of people and their relation one to another are more important than national distinctions. Mankind's chief problems, the problems of existence and peace, can only be solved by more students in continuing generations truly understanding and building on these two facts.

ANITA BROOKS

ACKNOWLEDGMENTS

Credit lines alone cannot fully convey my debt to the Food and Agriculture Organization (FAO), and to the photographic department of the United Nations Secretariat, both here in New York City and in Rome, Italy. Their kind availability, interest, and help with photographic material, information and statistics needs to be acknowledged not only in terms of gratitude but by an expression of admiration.

My appreciation goes to the many national consulate information bureaus who opened their photographic files to me, and, also, to those friends who helped me find photographs not always easily obtainable in these days of an uneasy, often fragmented world.

Special, long-delayed thanks are due the National Film Board of Canada, and Standard Oil of New Jersey, both of whom have been patient and generous in their photographic help throughout all the books in this series.

The Picture Book of Grains is dedicated to Amelia Zeltner and Ticia Stucklen. It is my hope they will read it together.

Anita Brooks

CONTENTS

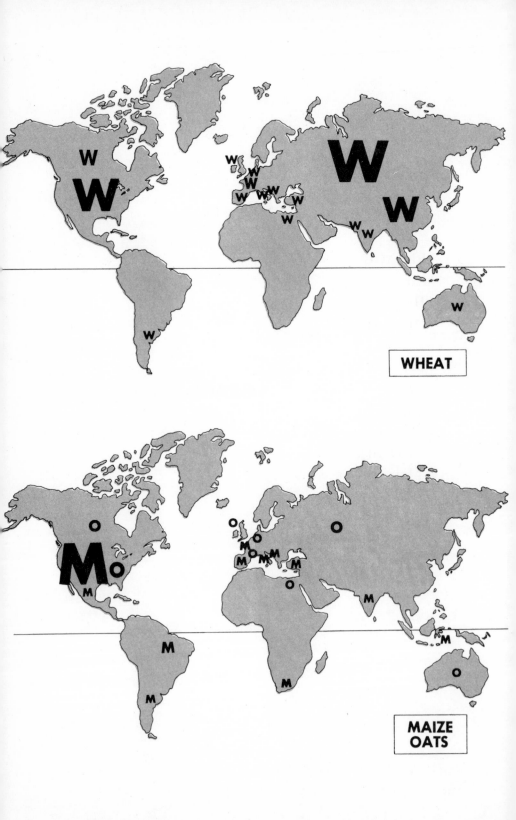

WHEAT

MAIZE
OATS

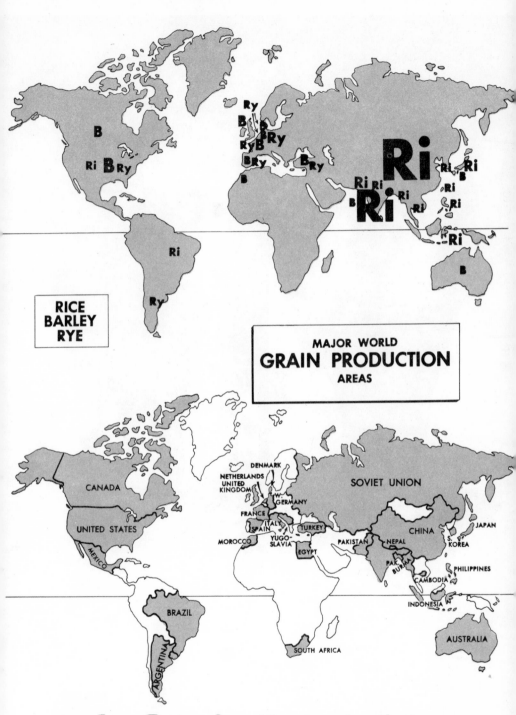

RICE
BARLEY
RYE

MAJOR WORLD
GRAIN PRODUCTION
AREAS

Map at lower right shows the world's major grain production areas. Other three maps show major areas producing particular kinds of grain. In each area, the larger the letter the greater the production.

THE LAND

Thousands of years ago man learned he could use the seeds of wild grasses for food. This knowledge changed his way of life. He stopped being a wanderer and a hunter, and became a grass farmer. The land took on a new meaning for him and the crops he grew became all-important to him. They fed him, his family, his work animals, and many other animals who gave him milk, eggs, meat, hides and wool. The dried grasses he used to make roofs to protect him from the rain and for bedding for himself and his animals. Today, these ancient crops are known as the cereal grasses: wheat, rye, oats, barley, maize (corn), rice, millet, and doura. The seeds of these grasses are called grain.

USDA Photo

This Indian farmer in the mountains of Bolivia, South America, is using one of man's earliest farming tools. It is called a foot plow.

In another part of South America, a small boy sits on new tractor machinery watching the team of oxen which up until now has helped his father plow the land. All over the world, old and new methods of farming are going on at the same time. One farmer, in one place, may be using an age-old wooden plow drawn by animals. At the same instant, another farmer may be plowing his land with a modern machine. At harvest time, some farmers will be cutting the crop with sickles (SIK-uls) or scythes (SYTHS). Others will be driving over prairies with machines called combines (KOM-bines) which do many jobs at once. This means that in different parts of the world there is a big difference in the amounts of grain farmers bring to markets. This difference can help make an area rich or keep it poor. Therefore, we say grain affects the *economy* (e-KON-oh-mi) of the world.

Trinidad & Tobago — Fritz Henle

Trinidad farmers plow a rice field using a wooden
plow and a team of water buffalo. The water buffalo is a member of the ox family.

This wide-horned water buffalo in Thailand does most of the
heavy work in the muddy rice fields. From oldest times, the
water buffalo has been the most important animal to farmers
in India, China, and much of the Orient.

USDA Photo

Australian News and Information

In Europe, particularly in Britain, oxen were the common plow animals until about 1800. Then the horse became the farmer's most dependable helper, and is still used on smaller farms in Europe, Australia, Argentina, Canada, and the United States.

13

The American Swedish News Exchange

Farm horses have large bones and broad feet, and are strong and powerful. They eat three times a day, so the farmer must plan to grow enough oats, barley or maize (corn) for their needs, too. He must also store hay (dried grass) for their food and bedding in the winter. Here, in Sweden, farm horses are drawing a plow. The little one stays close to his mother all day.

For hundreds of years farmers of small farms in Morocco have depended on this strange combination for work in the fields. Slowly, with help from such organizations as the Food and Agriculture Organization (FAO) of the United Nations, this method, which is hard on the animals and slow for the farmer, is being changed.

In Taiwan (Formosa), an aged rice farmer who has been used to the help of a water buffalo is being shown a power machine. He is being told that one machine can do the work of three water buffaloes. The machine does not eat grain or grass or need straw to sleep on, but it does use gasoline, needs new parts, and costs a lot of money. If this farmer uses it his whole way of life will change and this in turn will change ways of life in his village. So what the farmer decides is important.

The American Swedish News Exchange

The tractor has become the farmer's most important piece of machinery. He can hitch it to many different kinds of equipment. He uses it for clearing the land, for making soil ready for planting, for seeding, for cultivation, for cuttting the harvest, and for all the heavy farm work. Here, a farmer in Sweden uses a tractor to move a huge rock.

Sometimes a long period of bad weather will shorten the spring season. Then a farmer must work at night to plant thousands of acres as fast as possible. These farmers are working in the South of England.

British Information Services

A Norwegian farmer drives his tractor and disk harrow home along a dirt road in the spring countryside. The disk harrow is used for *tilling*. Tilling is the word used for breaking up the land and making it ready for seeding.

Norwegian Information Service

Much work is put into making the disks of a disk harrow. In a machine laboratory in Alabama, U.S.A., an engineer is making tests on disks to see which shapes are best for certain types of soil. Some disks are ground and polished by hand so they will be exactly the right cutting width. Others are polished by a special kind of blasting.

USDA Photo

More and more tractors are being made in factories around the world. These are some produced in Yugoslavia, a country which used to make most farming tools almost entirely by hand.

Not all farmers can afford to own their own tractors. In many countrysides, centers have been set
up where farmers can rent tractors, plows, and
other heavy machinery. Here, an Italian farmer is
arranging to hire a tractor by the hour.

United Nations

Here, under a government plan, about five hundred tractors are at work in all parts of the Union of Burma. The tractors are being used in the rice fields. These men keep track on a big board of where the tractors are working.

The way a farmer tills his land is important. Sometimes he plants different crops in straight, broad rows. Here, you can see how straight rows look on a farm in Japan.

Plowing in patterns that follow the slope of the land is called contour (KON-toor) plowing. Contour plowing helps keep topsoil from washing away. Here, strips of oats and grass planted on a slope in Wisconsin, U.S.A., show how contour plowing looks.

It is common practice among farmers to leave half of the vast acres of wheatland in the United States unplanted (fallow) throughout a growing season. The land will store up enough moisture for the following year's crops. This is summer fallow in Washington, U.S.A. Next year, these rolling hills will be covered with wheat.

Farmers fight many insects, crop diseases, and water and land problems. In Ohio, U.S.A., this gigantic boom on a specially built crop sprayer stretches 75 feet across the farmland. One man can spray 150 acres a day with this sprayer.

British Information Services

If you look closely you will see that these men in Hertfordshire, England, are not pouring something from a balloon. They are fixing up an insect trap which hangs from the balloon. The balloon will go into the sky and the trap which trails along will pull bugs out of the air. The men will study the bugs to find what kind of insects light on crops in certain types of weather.

Lack of all water is called *drought* (DROUT). Drought is feared by farmers all over the world. Here, in Libya, Africa, hundreds of sheep, donkeys and camels die of hunger and thirst in the droughts which strike the country every two or three years.

FAO Photo

The shifting and wearing away of soil is called *erosion* (e-ROH-zhun). Erosion is a constant problem for the farmer because it leaves large areas unfit for planting. Here, in southeast Australia, a soil conservation worker sprinkles straw on a bad section of land. A kind of cement will be sprayed on the straw to hold it together. This covering will give seeds planted underneath a chance to take hold. When the ground is once again covered by growing plants, the soil won't blow or slide away.

Australian News and Information

This fourteen-year-old boy is a field guard for the Department of Agriculture in Iraq. His job is to carry a stick with a heavy oval head. He uses it to kill snakes, frighten birds and drive away wandering animals.

USDA Photo

These are millions of tiny, dark insects called locusts. They are swarming in Ethiopia. They will eat every living green thing to the last blade of grass. Since biblical times, swarms of locusts have brought ruin and starvation to the farmer in countries ranging from India and China in the East to those parts of Africa which border on the South Atlantic Ocean.

FAO —
Desert Locust Survey

FAO Photo — Jean Manuel

This is a close-up of a type of desert locust. Man's fight against the locust goes on all the time. It is a difficult battle. Young locusts are hard to find. When they do move, they can travel up to 100 miles a day and can withstand temperatures that would kill other insects.

In Pakistan, a well-covered worker is spraying young locusts with poison. Other methods used to control locusts now include using airplanes to spray swarms in flight.

FAO Photo — W. Williams

The war with the locusts has become more and more an international effort. Through the work of the Food and Agriculture Organization (FAO) of the United Nations, fourteen of the countries most hurt by locusts were brought together to work on the problem. Special funds are used also to help carry on the study of the strange habits and movements of this deadly enemy of the farmer. Above, an Iranian flagman directs a plane spraying locusts, and, below, a desert police chief in Iraq reports where some young locusts can be found.

FAO Photo — Patrick Morin

Wheat is being harvested every month of the year some-
place in the world. It is grown in almost all countries
except the damp, hot tropics. The great wheat area lies
mostly in the northern hemisphere but wheat does well
also near the equator in the mountainous parts of Africa
and South America, and as far north as the Arctic Circle
or slightly beyond it.

THE HARVEST

Wheat is the most important of all cereal grains, because it makes the best bread. The wheat seed has a
dark outside called *bran*. The seed with the outside coat
is used to make whole wheat flour. The seed without the
bran is used to make white flour. There are many different types of wheat. A soft wheat is usually used for
pastry flour. Hard red wheats are used for bread. White
wheat is used for cereal breakfast foods. A wheat called
durum wheat is used in the making of spaghetti, macaroni, and noodles. Today, most flours are a combination
of different types of wheat blended together. Rye, below, looks much like wheat, but it is tougher and coarser.
It will grow on poorer soil and in damper regions. Its
main uses are for bread and livestock food. Large
amounts of rye are grown in Russia and Europe.

USDA Photo

USDA Photo

Oats can be grown in climates from the Gulf of Mexico to Alaska, but do best in the cooler, northern countries. Oats need less attention from the farmer than wheat, and the crop is easily harvested. Oats are used chiefly as a feed for livestock, but they are also a favorite breakfast cereal, and make good cookies and puddings. The straw makes good animal feed and bedding. Above, an oat field in Alaska is surrounded by snow-covered mountains.

USDA Photo

Bundles, called *sheaves* (SHEEVS), of oats are stacked for drying in a field in France.

Barley is one of the earliest known grains. It can be grown in temperate regions, as well as Asia Minor, Egypt, North Africa, India, and other tropical countries. It can also be grown in the extreme north, often within the Arctic Circle. Here is a fine field in Holland.

The National Film Board of Canada

Barley, like wheat, needs more care than some of the other grains. It is a good farm crop, though, because it ripens fast and can often be planted after a wheat or oat crop. Bread made from barley is not as good as that made from wheat, but barley is used in soups, as an animal feed, for the manufacture of malt for beer, and in the manufacture of commercial alcohol. Below, a three-horse team harvests oats and barley on Prince Edward Island, Canada.

A Galla farmer of Ethiopia cuts ripe wheat with a small sickle. The sickle is one of the earliest hand tools used for harvesting.

In the earliest days, man harvested grain by pulling up the plants by the roots. Then he used a hook to cut (*reap*) the grain. The reaping hook, in time, became a sickle, and the sickle grew to be a scythe. In 1806, a New England farmer invented the attachment shown in the picture. It is called a *cradle*. It is being used here in Morocco by a farmer scything (cutting down) his crops.

A young African farmer sharpens his scythe. Here
you can see how the cradle is attached. As the
grain is cut by the scythe, the cradle lays the stalks
straight for raking and binding.

Consulate General of Iceland

These two men are harvesting wheat in Iceland with a tractor and attachment.

Here a people's commune of Shenshi Province, China, works along with the machines to bring in the wheat harvest.

Hsinhwa News

Y. Ryumkin

The combine is one of the most advanced farm machines. Here, a combine operator at a machine and tractor station in the U.S.S.R. is showing a girl student how to drive the complex machine.

Much of the grain grown on the big farms in the Middle West of the United States is harvested by what is called "custom combining." Fleets of men and machines tour the farmlands and bring in the crops. Machines do all the work from cutting to bagging. The huge machines, which one farmer alone could not afford to own, can be seen here sweeping across a field in Nebraska, U.S.A.

Standard Oil Co., N. J.

The custom combine fleets carry their own repair trucks, their own supply trucks, and even eating and sleeping trailers for the men trained to run the machines. Here they are on the move, and, below, is the movable shop that fixes the machinery.

Standard Oil Co., N. J.

All farmland cannot be harvested by combine fleets.
They are practical only on large, flat prairies. Grain
that is not reaped by combine goes through several
stages of harvest. This harvest scene in England
shows grain stacked until ready for the next step —
threshing. Threshing is separating the grain seed
from the stalks.

43

Left, when a scythe is used for reaping, boys or women usually follow the reaper and bind up the fallen grain into bundles called *sheaves*. Sheaves are then put together in groups called *shocks* so that they will shed water when it rains. Grain is often reaped by machine. A machine does the work of many people. It cuts the wheat, binds it in bundles and ties the bundles with twine. Here are heads of grain which have been reaped and bound by a machine binder in France.

Grain stacks of many different shapes can be seen all over the world. Here is wheat in conelike piles in Colombia, South America.

USDA Photo

USDA Photo

On this farm in Holland, the rye stacks look like huts. The thatched roofs keep the grain dry until time for threshing. Threshing is done by machines that move through the countryside and do the job on many farms.

This is what barley looks like stacked on a hillside in Norway.

Norwegian Information Service

Bild Reportern — Bertil Nilsson

Here are some long, bumpy stacks of grain on a farm in Sweden.

All grain must be *threshed*. Threshing separates the grain seed from the stalk of grass. Wheat used to be threshed by animals tramping on it. Then farmers beat the wheat with sticks called *flails* (FLAYLS). Today, most wheat is threshed by a threshing machine such as the one farmers are watching at work here in Libya. Threshing is also done by combine machines which can cut, thresh and clean 60 acres of wheat in a single day.

FAO — Woodbridge Williams

In a small village in Ceylon, animals are still used in the old way to thresh rice. Their heavy hoofs will break and pound the stalks until the grain is free.

After threshing, grain must be cleaned (*winnowed* — WIN-ohed). The threshed grain is thrown into the air over and over again. The heavy kernels (KUR-nels) fall back to the ground and the bits of stalk and dust called *chaff* (CHAF) are blown away. On a state farm in An-hwei Province, China, workers are busy winnowing.

Hsinhwa News

Here in the Buenos Aires Province, Argentina, S.A., ripe wheat is ready for harvesting in the summer months which are from December to February. Wheat grows as far as the eye can see on the great prairie-like plains called *The Pampas*, where some of the great farms include tens of thousands of acres and where wheat farming is often combined with livestock ranching. Argentina is a leading producer of wheat, corn and *alfalfa*, a grass used for feeding cattle, horses, and other farm animals.

Australian News and Information

Here two modern machines do all the harvesting jobs right on the field. Barley is being bagged on a farm near Melbourne, Australia.

51

Spanish National Tourist News Bureau

These little huts in Spain, called *hórreos*, are for storing grain. They are raised on stone stilts to keep out rats and other animals. The villagers here make their living by fishing and farming. It is a combination way of earning a living found in many other small villages which are near the sea.

Left, trucks line up at a wheat silo in New South Wales, Australia. Farmers used to take grain straight to the mill for grinding into flour. Now it is stored in a farmer's own farm silo or in silos like these until it is sold and shipped away.

Australian News and Information — J. Tanner

FAO — Courtesy Toprak Ofisi

Some farmers haul their grain to buildings called
grain elevators and rent storage space there. This
modern granary (GRAN-uh-ri) in Turkey holds
20,000 tons.

Australian Department of Information

Big granaries are also sometimes called *terminals*. They are placed close to main waterways or railways for easy loading of the cars and boats that will take the grain to other countries. Shipping a product out of a country is called *exporting* it. Australia is one of the principal wheat exporting countries in the world. Others are Canada, the United States and Argentina.

Grain is transported by trucks, railroad cars, boats and airplanes. This shows how a car made especially to hold grain is loaded.

Australian News and Information

A grain boat is loaded from long pipes that shoot
the golden wheat into the holds of specially built
ships.

FAO Photo

Grain is examined and graded before it is sent to the mill or shipped out of a country. A grain sampler (above) makes a stab with a metal tube called a *probe* to get a sample from grain loaded in a railway car in Canada. Below, two members of a collective farm in the U.S.S.R. examine the quality of the grain before delivery to a grain elevator.

A. Skurikhin

Foto Sluzba Hrvatske

All the world has read about mills and millers in stories and poetry. These mills on the river Bosna in Yugoslavia are the remains of olden times. They are attached to the shore with chains and the rushing water of the river turns the lower end of a wheel underneath them. The windmill (below) is another kind of mill which uses the force of nature to turn machinery. There are not many of these mills in use anymore. This one is in southern Sweden.

The American Swedish News Exchange

FAO — Woodbridge Williams

Another old type of mill is one where animals walk-
ing round and round turn machinery that grinds
the grain into flour. This is a wheat mill of that
kind in Pakistan.

Malak, Ottawa

The inside of this modern Canadian mill is a maze of flour chutes. Wheat poured into the upper part of the mill is ground at different downward stages. Here, the miller is taking samples from small openings in the wooden chutes.

For thousands and thousands of years rice has
been the chief food of the people of Asia and the
Far East. Here, a Japanese girl eats rice from a
bowl.

There are many varieties of rice. Some 2,000 kinds are grown in India alone. Most rice is planted under water, but there are other types known as upland rice which can be grown on land not flooded. Rice is grown on coastal plains, deltas, and river basins in tropical, semitropical, and temperate regions where plenty of fresh water is close by. The crop is grown much the way wheat, oats and barley are grown except that the land is under water during most of the growing season. The principal rice-growing countries outside of the Orient are Egypt, Italy, Spain, Brazil, and the U.S.A. Rice is also grown in Yugoslavia, Greece, France, Africa, Australia, Ecuador, and British Guiana.

Usually when we think of riceland we think of rice terraces. Here are rice terraces in Java. But terracing is only one of many ways to grow rice, as you will see. Below, for example, rice called floating rice is being grown in deep water. This deepwater rice is growing on the Central Plain of Thailand. It reaches a height of 10 feet or more above floodwaters.

Here, in India, rice that is more fully grown makes
the terraces look more like a regular grainfield.

When rice is nearly ripe the water is drained off the fields so crops can be harvested. These men are harvesting rice in Louisiana, U.S.A. The rice grain (kernel) has many thin layers or coats to protect it. After harvesting these layers will need to be removed.

Here, in France, a combine machine is harvesting the rice.

As soon as the rainy season ends, a rice farmer
must start weeding the fields. This farmer is working in his rice field in Japan. Much rice in Asia and
the Far East is grown on small farms by many
millions of farmers.

Rice can be seeded by hand or by airplane. Here, in Texas, U.S.A., an airplane is broadcasting rice seed in fields flooded for planting. Below, planting by hand in the rice fields of the Kocani plains of Yugoslavia.

FAO Photo

Rice must be planted again after the seed has grown into small shoots. This is called *transplanting*. The small shoots are placed in even rows. This is often done by hand (above), or with planting machines like those below.

Hsinhwa News

FAO Photo — Eric Schwab

Harvested rice must be dried before threshing.
Here, in Sarawak, which is next to the northwest
coast of Borneo, a mat of drying rice is being protected from birds by a young girl with a swinging
pole.

A Malayan farmer is threshing rice by beating it against a woven mat. The beating will break up the stalks and the grain seed will fall down into the little chute into the basket below. This is only one of many different ways of threshing rice.

Here, in Liberia, the rice has been dried in the huts in the background, and is now being threshed in a machine. After threshing, rice is milled. When the milling is done by hand, the rice is pounded over and over again. Today, around the world, machines have taken the place of hand pounding.

In Asia and the Orient, the rice field and the rice itself are both called *paddy*. Above, Burmese girls are tossing paddy into the air. They will do this over and over again until the rice kernel is free from all the dust, dirt and broken straw left from the threshing. This is called *winnowing*. Below, two girls in Malaya use a basket hung from a pole to help them winnow the rice.

This is the inside of a rice storage shed in New South Wales, Australia. The pipes are there to bring in and keep air moving. It is important to control the amount and movement of air inside a rice storage room so the rice grain will not crack.

These bags of rice are being unloaded and stacked on a dock in Puerto Rico. They are an *import* to Puerto Rico. In other words, the rice was grown outside Puerto Rico and then shipped from the country that grew it as an *export* from that country. This is the way an export becomes an import. *Import* means to bring in for sale or use. This imported rice will now be transported to different parts of Puerto Rico and sold there to the people, who will use it for food.

These men, on a river in Minnesota, U.S.A., have
harvested wild rice and the man who is buying the
rice has set up his scales right on the spot. Wild
rice grows in only a few places so this man will
pay a very high price for the rice. By the time the
wild rice reaches the stores, it will sell for several
dollars a pound.

In Europe and the Americas the word "corn" has two different meanings. In Europe it is used when speaking of the leading cereal crop of a district. In England, it would refer to wheat; in Scotland and Ireland, to oats; and in certain parts of northern Europe, to rye or barley. In the U.S.A. and South America, the word "corn" is used only for the grain the rest of the world calls "maize." When talking about this grain around the world, maize is the best word to use. Europeans have another name for maize. They sometimes call it "Indian corn" because it was a plant grown by American Indians and introduced into Europe by Columbus. The height of a maize stalk may be almost as short as a ruler, or as high as a one-story house. The United States produces about half the world's crop of maize, and Argentina, S.A., ranks second.

FAO — Courtesy of the Rockefeller Foundation

Maize is used as a feed for livestock, for human food, and for raw materials in industry. It makes cornstarch, corn sugar, corn syrup, corn oil, and industrial alcohol. Stalks make paper and wallboard. Corncobs are used for fuel and making charcoal, and for making corncob pipes. Here a farmer in India stands in his field of maize, a type developed in the United States.

Here seeds of commonly grown types of maize have been sent to Italy from the U.S.A. to be tested on different kinds of land in that country to see whether they will be right for Italian soil and farming methods. This is done through the Food and Agriculture Organization (FAO) of the United Nations. Below, in South America, where Argentina is the leading producer of maize, a worker is mixing seeds of different types of maize in tests to develop new and better crops. This kind of testing and exchange goes on all over the world.

Maize, like the other grains, is sometimes harvested and made ready for use or for sale entirely by hand labor, and sometimes all the steps are done by machines. Above, a farmer on a small farm in El Salvador, Central America, beats the maize to break the kernels off the cobs. This is called *flailing*. Below can be seen some of the machines used in grading and testing corn kernels.

Maize must be protected from rats and other animals, so it is usually stored in metal containers, sometimes called *cribs*, like the one above.

Farmers in out-of-the-way places in the world sometimes store their maize in trees. Here, a farmer in Nepal has put his crop high and safe for winter.

Maize is used to make flat cakes called *tortillas*, and for corn bread, hominy, mush, breakfast cereals, and popcorn. It is also eaten as the vegetable we call "corn." Here, in Guatemala, Central America, tortillas are being made in the old-fashioned way. These women have made the flour themselves from the maize, and now they are cooking the cakes.

Farmers near Chryssoupolis, Greece, are collecting straw. Straw is the dried stems or stalks of cereal grasses. Straw is now used in many important industries: mat making, stuffing of bedding, weaving of hats, making baskets, making pulp for paper, and for protection of glass and china in transport. For straw, the wheat crop is usually mowed by hand with sickles or scythes.

Indian farmers gathering straw. This straw will be used for thatching roofs and feeding animals.

Straw is sometimes used to keep rain off the farmer himself. Here is a fancy, but practical, raincoat made of straw used by some of the farmers in Portugal.

FAO Photo

This man is frightening birds away from the millet fields in Ethiopia. Millet is an ancient grass. It has been cultivated since earliest times in Asia and Egypt, and is now widely grown in Russia, southern Europe, and the Orient. Millet is an important source of food in India, China, Japan, and parts of Europe and Africa. It is also good feed for chickens and other poultry.

These are heads of a grain called *doura*. This crop is sun-drying after a harvest in Yemen. Doura is an important farm animal feed in many parts of the world.

STUDY AND EXCHANGE

The plant breeder, the scientist, the manufacturer of machinery, the weather expert, the conservation worker, and the teacher are all important to the farmer. Through the Food and Agriculture Organization (FAO) of the United Nations many different kinds of knowledge and many skills are exchanged around the world. Practical help is also given directly to farmers. Below, a teacher in Burma uses a blackboard to give a tractor-driving lesson.

United Nations

British Information Services

The plant breeder is to agriculture what the inventor
is to industry. Here, in England, a plant breeder
looks over some barley plants. Britain's interest in
agricultural science is very keen. She has no land to
waste and must make the best use of all her countryside.

These are truly atomic-age testing machines in a laboratory in England. Chemists here use radioactive isotopes to study how fertilizers work on plants, and to make many other plant tests.

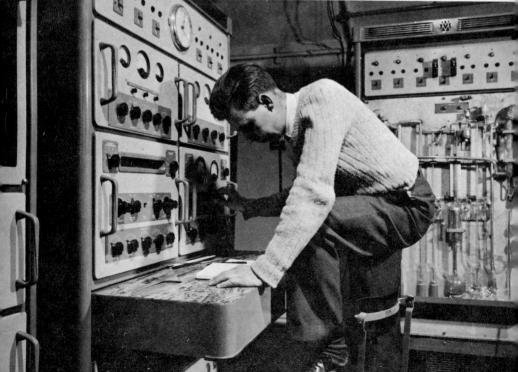

In Japan a new type of tractor made especially for rice fields is tried out by a man with special knowledge about tractors.

This flour is on its way to a part of the world which has been stricken with starvation (famine). The sacks here have been given by more than 20 countries in answer to a request by the Food and Agriculture Organization (FAO), and they are being sent by plane as part of a United Nations' program of help in emergencies. Other food stuffs and, most important of all, fertilizer, seed, hoes, and other simple tools will be sent also so that the starving people will be able to plant new crops right away.

This is a seed test being carried out under glass in the Netherlands. The glass covers are called "Copenhagen tanks." On the right, in Tunisia, a Food and Agriculture Organization (FAO) expert from China has developed a simple method of taking salt from the land so rice can be grown. This can make an important change for Tunisia. The country may be able someday soon to grow all its own rice and not have to bring any from outside. Here, the expert is checking the results of a water experiment.

Weather conditions are important to the farmer.
Here, a man from the United Nations who knows a
great deal about weather is checking and studying
conditions in a maize field in Israel.

These two men know all about drilling to find water. One is from UNESCO and is a Frenchman, the other is from Brazil. They are testing soil in an area where there has been lack of water.

A class at a village community center in Java, Indonesia, shows rice farmers how to improve the water supply in their own fields.

Our "daily bread" has many different forms, but is eaten
by all peoples of the world. It may be a loaf of rye or
white bread. It may be an enormous, round, dark loaf
from Hungary, or the thin, long French or Italian breads.
It may be paper-thin wafers from Arabia, folded like a
book. You eat a page at a time. It may be Norwegian
bread, looking like a pancake or a large cracker. It may be
flat cakes made of rice or corn. It can be cereal (hot or
cold). It may be twisted rings like these in a basket in
Portugal. It may be tortillas of corn, or it may be macaroni, or spaghetti. It may be different kinds of noodles. What-
ever form it takes, grain is still man's most important food.

INDEX

Africa, 30, 34, 38, 61
  See also Egypt, Ethiopia, Liberia, Libya, Morocco, Tunisia
Alaska, *see* U.S.A.
Alfalfa, 50
Animals (Farm), 8, 15
  Horses, 13, 14
  Oxen, 11, 13
  Water buffalo, 12, 16
Arabian bread, 94
Arctic Circle, 30, 34
Argentina, 13, 50, 54, 75, 77
Asia, 60, 65, 71, 83
  See also Burma, Ceylon, China, Formosa, Indonesia, India, Iran, Iraq, Israel, Japan, Malaya, Nepal, Pakistan, Sarawak, Thailand, Turkey, U.S.S.R., Yemen
Asia Minor, 34
Australia, 13, 26, 50, 52, 54, 61, 72

Barley, 9, 14, 34, 35, 46, 50, 61, 75
Bolivia, 10
Brazil, 61
Bread, *see* Flour
Britain, *see* England
Burma, 21, 71, 85

Canada, 13, 35, 54, 56, 59
Central America, 78, 80
  See also Ecuador, El Salvador, Guatemala
Ceylon, 49
China (Chinese People's Republic), 12, 27, 39, 49, 83
China (Nationalist), *see* Formosa
Colombia, 45

Combines, *See* Machinery (Farm)
Conservation, 26
Contour Plowing, 23
Corn, *see* Maize
Cradle, 37, 38

Doura, 9, 84
Drought, 26

Economy, 11
Ecuador, 61
Egypt, 34, 61, 83
El Salvador, 78
England, 13, 17, 25, 43, 75, 86, 87
Ethiopia, 27, 36, 83
Europe, 13, 31, 75, 83
  See also England, France, Greece, Holland, Iceland, Ireland, Italy, Netherlands, Norway, Portugal, Scotland, Spain, Sweden, U.S.S.R., Yugoslavia
Erosion, 26
Export, 54, 73

FAO, 15, 29, 77, 85, 88, 89, 90
Flour, 31, 52, 58, 59, 80, 89
  Bread, 31, 35, 80, 94
  Macaroni, 31, 94
  Noodles, 31, 94
  Spaghetti, 31, 94
  Tortilla, 80, 94
Formosa, 16
France, 33, 45, 61, 64

Grain elevators, 53, 54, 56
Grain boat, 55
Greece, 61, 81

Guatemala, 80

Hay, 14
Holland, 34, 46
Hungarian bread, 94

Iceland, 39
Import, 73, 90
India, 12, 27, 34, 61, 63, 76, 81, 83
Indonesia, 62, 93
Iran, 29
Iraq, 27, 29
Ireland, 75
Isotopes, 87
Israel, 92
Italy, 20, 61, 77, 94

Japan, 22, 60, 65, 83, 88

Liberia, 70
Locusts, 27, 28, 29
Libya, 26, 48

Macaroni, *see* Flour
Machinery (Farm)
    Combines, 11, 40, 41, 42, 43, 48, 64
    Crop sprayer, 24
    Disk harrow, 18
    Insect trap, 25
    Plows, 10, 14, 20
    Tractors, 11, 16, 17, 19, 20, 21, 39, 88
Maize (Corn), 9, 14, 50, 75, 76, 77, 78, 79, 80, 92
Malaya, 69, 71
Millet, 9, 83
Morocco, 15, 37

Nepal, 79
Netherlands, 90
Noodles, *see* Flour
Norway, 18, 46, 94

Oats, 9, 14, 23, 32, 33, 35, 61, 75
Orient, 12, 60, 61, 65, 71
    See also Asia

Paddy, *see* Rice
Pampas (The), 50
Pakistan, 28, 58

Plow, *see* Machinery (Farm)
Portugal, 82, 94
Probe, 56
Puerto Rico, 73

Rice, 9, 12, 16, 21, 60, 61, 62, 63, 64, 65, 66, 67, 68, 69, 70, 71, 72, 73, 90, 93
Rye, 9, 31, 46, 75

Sarawak, 68
Scotland, 75
Scythe, 11, 37, 38, 45, 81
Sheaves, 33, 45
Shocks, 45, 46, 47
Sickle, 11, 36, 37, 81
South America, 11, 30, 75
    See also Argentina, Bolivia, Brazil, Colombia
Spaghetti, *see* Flour
Spain, 51, 61
Straw, 81, 82
Sweden, 14, 17, 47

Thailand, 12, 62
Threshing, 43, 46, 48, 49, 68, 69, 70
Tilling, 18, 22
Topsoil, 23
Tortillas, 80, 94
Tractor, *see* Machinery (Farm)
Trinidad, 12
Tunisia, 90
Turkey, 53

United Nations, 92, 93
    See also FAO
U.S.A., 13, 18, 23, 24, 41, 54, 61, 64, 66, 74, 75, 76, 77
    Alaska, 32
U.S.S.R. (Russia), 31, 40, 56, 83

Wheat, 9, 23, 30, 31, 32, 35, 36, 39, 45, 48, 50, 52, 54, 55, 58, 59, 61, 75, 81
Wild Rice, 74
Winnowing, 49, 71

Yemen, 84
Yugoslavia, 19, 57, 61, 66